A Book for Women, Mostly

3 Quick and Easy Steps
For Strengthening Your Marriage!

Randall Krug, M.A.

Krug Haus Publishing

Dedication

This practical approach for improving relationships is dedicated to the men and women who reviewed, questioned, supported, nudged, worked through the book, sat in multiple focus groups and participated in pilot seminars. Their efforts have helped create resources for individuals and couples to use in their most important relationship.

Other books by Randall Krug
3 Quick and Easy Steps for Strengthening Your Marriage
A Book for Men, Mostly
3QES – Connections Folder
Communications Tool Kit

www.lulu.com/spotlight/krughauspublishing

Contents

Setting the Stage

This book grew out my professional background, as well as research regarding relationships and human behavior. *A Book for Women, Mostly* aims at meeting a clearly defined need for many people: immediate help in their relationship and life.

During my career, I facilitated communication and leadership seminars nationally and internationally for such organizations as Arthur Andersen & Co., AT&T, Boise-Cascade, the Joint Commission on Accreditation of Hospitals, State Farm Insurance and the University of Michigan. Topics included setting direction, planning, communication skills, social styles, conflict management, problem solving, goal writing, managing change and many more.

Several years ago, at the conclusion of a weeklong leadership seminar I delivered in Boston, two participants approached me and asked, "Have you ever thought about using some of the seminar content to help people in relationships?" That's when it hit me! Communication and leadership content could be helpful in relationships and affect individuals, couples and families in positive ways. It was time to act.

Through on-going research, and hundreds of interviews, I found that people were looking for information in several areas of their relationships: confirmation that they were already doing certain things well, some much needed inspiration, proven resources and easy-to-use tools to help in their relationship.

The information I gathered also indicated that the final product needed to be direct, a quick read and concrete. People wanted to spend their time on action instead of wading through pages of dense text. As these materials evolved, psychologists and social workers checked the content, it held up. Many men and women reviewed the early drafts or participated in focus groups and provided feedback on the layout and content. When the book started to expand, they said, "Keep it simple," and the text returned to basic ideas. Everyone involved gave the book two thumbs up!

As a result, the content of each book reflects a solution-driven approach that builds on the good already present in a marriage and provides proven tools to support the on-going success of individuals and couples in strengthening their relationships.

The outcome of the original question about applying leadership and communication content to couples, produced three educational resources for men and women in relationships:
- *3 Quick and Easy Steps for Strengthening Your Marriage*
- A *Book for Men, Mostly*
- *A Book for Women, Mostly*

About Randall Krug

Randall Krug's bold ideas have created breakthrough solutions for individuals and couples who are looking for ideas to help their relationship. He created self-customized learning resources for people to overcome the day-to-day challenges they face.

Randall is a veteran of the United States Navy and attended Michigan State University where he graduated with a degree in education, and again from MSU with a master's degree in instructional design, the practice of arranging content to help people learn most effectively.

For the next 20 years, Randall dedicated his life to creating self-customized learning resources and delivering practical and meaningful seminars. His goal continues to be providing learning resources to help people improve their lives and thereby the lives of others.

Content experts and focus group members all said, it was a pleasure to review the content of this book and find a resource that is straight forward, simplified and useful immediately.

Randall's career leading communication and leadership seminars in national and international business, non-profit organizations and consulting, helped hone the accountability of the content and sharpen his delivery. He is an entertaining, inspiring and insightful writer and seminar leader.

3 Quick and Easy Steps at a Glance

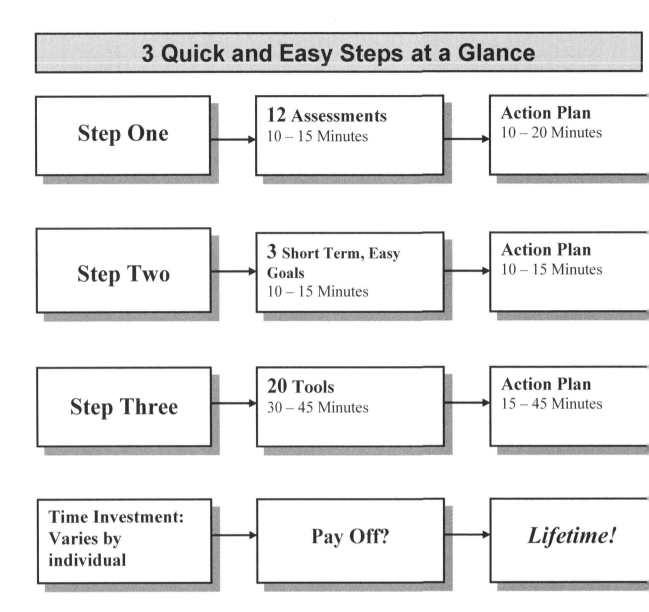

| Step One | **12** Assessments
10 – 15 Minutes | **Action Plan**
10 – 20 Minutes |

| Step Two | **3** Short Term, Easy Goals
10 – 15 Minutes | **Action Plan**
10 – 15 Minutes |

| Step Three | **20** Tools
30 – 45 Minutes | **Action Plan**
15 – 45 Minutes |

| **Time Investment:**
Varies by
individual | **Pay Off?** | *Lifetime!* |

3 Quick and Easy Steps Diagram

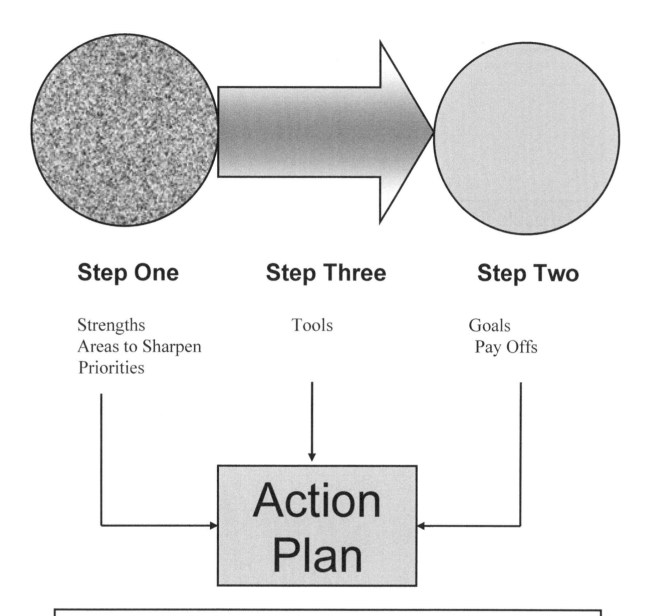

Step One   **Step Three**   **Step Two**

Strengths   Tools   Goals
Areas to Sharpen   Pay Offs
Priorities

Action Plan

The diagram shows the sequence for creating an Action Plan. Step One is a snapshot of how your marriage is today. The key is that it identifies strengths already present in your marriage to allow you to **build on good**.

The second step is to write 3 goals and their pay offs. Step Three is selecting from a set of proven tools those that will take you from where you are today toward the future you've outlined in your goals.

Each of these steps will be transferred to your one-page Action Plan.

"If we could first know where we are, and whither we are drifting, we could better judge what to do and how to do it."
Abraham Lincoln

Step One

Identifying Your Strengths, Areas to Sharpen and Setting Priorities

Starting Point: Your Marriage Today

Instructions

12 Assessments
1. Chemistry
2. Interests
3. Communication
4. Social Compatibility
5. Intimacy
6. Point of View
7. Money
8. Self-Care
9. Meeting Needs
10. Underlying Currents
11. Quiet Moments
12. Our History Together

Completing Your Action Plan
- Strengths
- Areas to Sharpen
- Setting Priorities

Where Do I Go From Here?
- Taking Control
- Clear Direction

Starting Point: Your Marriage Today

You've made a decision to improve the most important relationship in your life: your marriage.

In Step One, you'll rediscover the strengths already present in your marriage, pinpoint areas to sharpen and set your priorities for moving forward.

It may take time and there may be some speed bumps, but the best thing you can do right now, like so many other women, is take that first step.

Therefore:
- Start now.
- Build on strengths.
- Get the momentum going.

Instructions

There are 12 assessment exercises in Step One. Each has a set of 5 questions. They can be answered by circling Y, S, or N: Yes... Sometimes... No.

Go through these 12 assessments by yourself, not with your husband. Each assessment will give you an indication of how you think your marriage is today. That means right now, today, not how you'd like it to be in the future.

When you've completed all 12 assessments, you'll transfer your results to your Action Plan. Additionally, at that time, you'll be able to identify what you believe to be your strengths.

Read the questions carefully, some are about you and others include you and your husband.

The 12 assessments are not deep analytical reviews, but they do serve as a snapshot of your marriage today.

Common Sense
When completing each of the assessments, it's important that you use common sense, along with the assessment results, to determine if the topic is a Strength or an Area to Sharpen. At the bottom of the page add up your Ys and write the total in Strengths. Add the Ss and Ns and write the number in Areas to Sharpen.

Usually 3 Ys will make the assessment a Strength, 2 Ys an S and an N would usually be an Area to Sharpen. However, when you apply your common sense, what came out in an Area to Strengthen may become a Strength. Or, you may have enough Ys for a Strength, but common sense, and your own experience, might tell you it's an Areas to Sharpen.

At the end of Step One, transfer your results to your Action Plan.

Estimated time to complete Step One: 10 – 25 minutes.

1. Chemistry

Read the questions. Circle Y, S or N ("Yes", "Sometimes" or "No").

1.	Are you physically attracted to your husband?	Y S N
2.	Is there something you can't explain that draws you to him, like a magnet?	Y S N
3.	Do you still get that excited feeling in your stomach, knowing you'll see him soon?	Y S N
4.	Is it still fun to surprise him with something nice?	Y S N
5.	Do you look forward to being intimate?	Y S N

Total Ys = _____ Strength
Total S + N = _____ An Area to Sharpen

Based on your assessments and common sense,
Chemistry is a Strength_____ or An Area to Sharpen_____.

2. Interests

Read the questions. Circle Y, S or N ("Yes", "Sometimes" or "No").

1. Do you like many of the same recreational activities?   Y S N

2. Do you feel OK when your husband pursues his interests without you?   Y S N

3. Do you feel OK when you're pursuing your interests without him?   Y S N

4. Do you get a good feeling doing "things" together?   Y S N

5. Do you enjoy finding new common interests?   Y S N

Total Ys = _____ Strength
Total S + N = _____ An Area to Sharpen

Based on your assessments and common sense,
Interests is a Strength_____or An Area to Sharpen_____.

3. Communication

Read the questions. Circle Y, S or N ("Yes", "Sometimes" or "No").

1. Do you really listen to your husband?   Y S N

2. Are the discussions between the two of you balanced?   Y S N

3. In everyday conversation, do you give him complete information about a topic, or do you hold back because you're concerned with how he'll react?   Y S N

4. Do you feel good at the end of your discussions?   Y S N

5. Are you comfortable talking with your husband about a variety of topics?   Y S N

Total Ys = _____ Strength
Total S + N = _____An Area to Sharpen

Based on your assessments and common sense,
Communication is a Strength_____or An Area to Sharpen_____.

4. Social Compatibility

Read the questions. Circle Y, S or N ("Yes", "Sometimes" or "No").

1.	Do you enjoy mutual friends?	Y S N
2.	Is your sense of humor similar?	Y S N
3.	Are your social interests in sync with his?	Y S N
4.	Do you and your husband have similar outlooks in grooming and appearance?	Y S N
5.	Do you feel comfortable when you're out in public together?	Y S N

Total Ys = _____ Strength
Total S + N = _____An Area to Sharpen

Based on your assessments and common sense,
Social Compatibility is a Strength_____or An Area to Sharpen_____.

5. Intimacy

Read the questions. Circle Y, S or N ("Yes", "Sometimes" or "No").

1.   Do you feel complete when you're with your husband?   Y S N

2.   Do you often think romantically about him?   Y S N

3.   Do you feel a deep emotional connection with him?   Y S N

4.   Do you have confidence in the trust between you?   Y S N

5.   Do you honor his reality?   Y S N

Total Ys = _____ Strength
Total S + N = _____ An Area to Sharpen

Based on your assessments and common sense,
Intimacy is a Strength_____ or An Area to Sharpen_____.

6. Point of View

Read the questions. Circle Y, S or N ("Yes", "Sometimes" or "No").

Are you and your husband's views basically in sync regarding?

1.	Education	Y S N
2.	Entertainment	Y S N
3.	Politics	Y S N
4.	Spirituality	Y S N
5.	Parenting	Y S N

Total Ys = _____ Strength
Total S + N = _____An Area to Sharpen

Based on your assessments and common sense,
Point of View is a Strength_____or An Area to Sharpen_____.

7. Money

Read the questions. Circle Y, S or N ("Yes", "Sometimes" or "No").

1. Do you and your husband have similar views on
   spending money?   Y S N

2. Do you live within your financial means?   Y S N

3. Do you make financial plans together?   Y S N

4. Are you able to discuss financial concerns
   constructively?   Y S N

5. Do you both agree on the financial roles each
   of you play?   Y S N

Total Ys = _____ Strength
Total S + N = _____ An Area to Sharpen

Based on your assessments and common sense,
Money is a Strength_____ or An Area to Sharpen_____.

8. Self Care

Read the questions. Circle Y, S or N ("Yes", "Sometimes" or "No").

In your opinion, do you both:

1.	Have similar beliefs about nutrition?	Y S N
2.	Plan medical and dental visits as part of your approach to health?	Y S N
3.	Agree on exercise and fitness?	Y S N
4.	Get enough rest and sleep to be refreshed?	Y S N
5.	Stay away from addictions?	Y S N

Total Ys = _____ Strength
Total S + N = _____ An Area to Sharpen

Based on your assessments and common sense,
Self Care is a Strength_____ or An Area to Sharpen_____.

9. Meeting Needs

Read the questions. Circle Y, S or N ("Yes", "Sometimes" or "No").

1.   Do you let your husband know you're proud of him?   Y S N

2.   Do you give your husband affection everyday?   Y S N

3.   Do you take the necessary steps to make sure
     he can relax?   Y S N

4.   Do you try to fulfill his intimacy needs?   Y S N

5.   At the end of the day do you think he really
     knows you care about him?   Y S N

Total Ys = _____ Strength
Total S + N = _____ An Area to Sharpen

Based on your assessments and common sense,
Meeting Needs is a Strength_____ or An Area to Sharpen_____.

10. Underlying Currents

Read the questions. Circle Y, S or N ("Yes", "Sometimes" or "No").

1.	Is your mind free of old thoughts that can interfere with your marriage moving forward?	Y S N
2.	Do you talk openly with your husband about what's going on in your tummy?	Y S N
3.	Is your marriage your top priority?	Y S N
4.	Do you try to create a positive atmosphere for your marriage to grow?	Y S N
5.	Do you sincerely care about your husband's well being?	Y S N

Total Ys = _____ Strength
Total S + N = _____An Area to Sharpen

Based on your assessments and common sense,
Underlying Currents is a Strength_____or An Area to Sharpen_____.

11. Quiet Moments

Read the questions. Circle Y, S or N ("Yes", "Sometimes" or "No").

1. In the early morning hours, when he's
    asleep and you're lying awake, does it
    bring out feelings in you of protection and caring?   Y S N

2. Does traditional time together, such as reading the
    Sunday paper over a second cup of coffee or going
    to a special Friday night movie, give you a feeling
    of contentment?   Y S N

3. When you make eye contact across a room at a
    function or party, is it a good feeling?   Y S N

4. At a movie, concert or sporting event, there's that
    "settling in feeling" just before it starts. Do you
    get a positive feeling being with him?   Y S N

5. At weddings, funerals and religious services, are
    you glad you're with your husband?   Y S N

Total Ys = _____ Strength
Total S + N = _____ An Area to Sharpen

Based on your assessments and common sense,
Quiet Moments is a Strength_____ or An Area to Sharpen_____.

12. Our History Together

Read the questions. Circle Y, S or N ("Yes", "Sometimes" or "No").

1. Can you remember the first time you saw your husband?   Y S N

2. Have you had good times together?   Y S N

3. Have you helped each other get through some tough
    times?   Y S N

4. Have you helped each other adjust to changes?   Y S N

5. Do you get a good feeling when you recall your
    history together?   Y S N

Total Ys = _____ Strength
Total S + N = _____An Area to Sharpen

Based on your assessments and common sense,
Our History Together is a Strength_____or An Area to Sharpen_____.

Identifying Your Strengths, Areas to Sharpen and Setting Priorities

Look at the bottom of each page for the 12 Assessments.

1. **Strengths:** on your Action Plan circle the corresponding **S** for each of your strengths. The remaining assessments are An Area to Sharpen.

2. The next activity will help you set your priorities.

3. **An Area to Sharpen:**
   a. Will working on this topic be Easy or Difficult? Place an X on the corresponding line on your Action Plan.
   b. Will the Pay Off for improving this topic be Big or Small? Place an X on the corresponding line on your Action Plan.

4. Use the Priority Scale below to identify your priorities and mark each Area to Sharpen a 1, 2, 3 or 4 on the priority scale.

Priority Scale

Easy + Big	= 1
Easy + Small	= 2
Difficult + Big	= 3
Difficult + Small	= 4

5. Your priorities do not reflect the most important areas to strengthen but they are the easiest to work on with the greatest pay off. That will create more positives to build upon and generate momentum.

6. The example on the page at the right shows an Action Plan with Step One completed.

Estimated time to complete Step One of your Action Plan: 10 - 20 minutes.

Identifying My Strengths, Areas to Sharpen and Setting Priorities

	Strengths	Areas To Sharpen		Priorities
		Working on this will be: EASY/Difficult	The pay off will be: BIG/Small	
1. Chemistry	(S)	__/__	__/__	___
2. Interests	S	X/__	__/X	_2_
3. Communication	S	_X/__	__/X_	_2_
4. Social Compatibility	S	__/X	__/X	_4_
5. Intimacy	(S)	__/__	__/__	___
6. Point of View	S	X/__	X/__	_1_
7. Money	(S)	__/__	__/__	___
8. Self-Care	S	__/X	__/X	_4_
9. Meeting Needs	S	__/X	X/__	_3_
10. Underlying Currents	S	__/X	X/__	_3_
11. Quiet Moments	S	__/X_	X/__	_3_
12. Our History	(S)	__/__	__/__	___

This person has three strengths:
- Chemistry
- Money
- Our History Together

1. Her number **one** priority is:
- Point of View

2. There are two, number **two** priorities:
- Interests
- Communications

3. There are three number **three** priorities:
- Meeting Needs
- Underlying Currents
- Quiet Moments

4. There are two number **four** priorities:
- Social Compatibility
- Self-Care

This example will also be used in Steps Two and Three

Complete Step One of Your Action Plan

1. Review the results of your 12 assessments.

2. Circle the corresponding strengths on your Action Plan.

3. For each Area to Sharpen, select Easy or Difficult to work on.

4. For each Area to Sharpen, decide if it will have a Big or Small pay off.

5. Use the Priority Scale below to set your priorities.

Priority Scale

Easy + Big   = 1
Easy + Small   = 2
Difficult + Big   = 3
Difficult + Small   = 4

6. Double check your assessments to make sure it's what you truly believe.

Step One - Action Plan

Identifying My Strengths, Areas to Sharpen and Setting Priorities

	Strengths	Areas To Sharpen		Priorities
		Working on this will be: EASY/Difficult	The pay off will be: BIG/Small	
1. Chemistry	S	__/__	__/__	__
2. Interests	S	__/__	__/__	__
3. Communication	S	__/__	__/__	__
4. Social Compatibility	S	__/__	__/__	__
5. Intimacy	S	__/__	__/__	__
6. Point of View	S	__/__	__/__	__
7. Money	S	__/__	__/__	__
8. Self Care	S	__/__	__/__	__
9. Meeting Needs	S	__/__	__/__	__
10. Underlying Currents	S	__/__	__/__	__
11. Quiet Moments	S	__/__	__/__	__
12. Our History	S	__/__	__/__	__

Priority Scale

Easy + Big	= 1
Easy + Small	= 2
Difficult + Big	= 3
Difficult + Small	= 4

Where Do I Go From Here?

Taking Control

Most women don't slow down long enough to get a clear snapshot of how their marriage is today. You just did.

That means you took control of your marriage and your future. Whatever the results are on your Action Plan, you've begun.

Again, the 12 assessments are not intended to be a comprehensive survey and analysis of your marriage. The assessments are a straight forward quick and easy way to get a sense of where you are in your marriage today, perhaps recalling some positives that may have slipped into the back of your mind.

As you went through the 12 assessments you either confirmed or rediscovered Strengths. These will become the foundation upon which you can build. Keep at it; stay focused.

Summary: You're building on good.

Clear Direction

Now that you have a picture of where your marriage is today, Step Two, Creating Three Short-Term, Easy Goals That Support Your Priorities will help you frame out a clear and immediate direction for your future.

Step Two

Creating 3 Short-Term, Easy Goals that Support Your Priorities

Starting Point: Setting Your Direction

Instructions

Short-Term Easy Goals
- Short Term
- Easy Goals
- Pay Offs

Completing Your Action Plan
- 3 Short-Term Easy Goals That Support Your Priorities

Where Do I Go From Here?
- Checking Your Progress
- Selecting the Right Tools to Reach Your Goals

Starting Point: Setting Your Direction

Some call planning for your future, a personal vision. Others label it a personal mission statement. We'll call it Setting Your Direction. That means reviewing the results of Step One and in your mind's eye creating a picture of how you'd like your marriage to be in the future. Setting Your Direction, through clear meaningful goals, is a critical step in realizing that future. And it all starts now!

Keep building the momentum for improving your marriage by focusing your efforts on just a few high pay off areas at a time.

It's important to note that working through this book is about you, not your husband. He'll react to the changes you make.

Therefore:
- You're 50% in charge of your relationship
- You're 100% in charge of what you do.

Creating 3 Short-Term, Easy Goals that Support Your Priorities

It's common for women to write goals relating to work or sports or the home, for example, or at least think about goals. Usually the goals include an action verb, time frame and a way of measuring the goal.

When you write your goals you'll begin to define your future.

The results of Step One outline where your marriage is strong today, and what you see as a Strength. With that information, you then identified your priorities to gain momentum.

You'll see one critical difference when writing these goals: pay off.

The measurable part of your goals will be the pay off. In other words, the pay off will describe what you'll experience when you reach your goals, i.e., the benefits. Writing down the pay offs helps you visualize how your goals translate into real action.

Estimated time to complete Step Two: 10 – 15 minutes.

Short-Term, Easy Goals

What does Short Term mean?

Short term means your goals are attainable within a week or two. It does not mean stretching out the time frame of your goals six months into the future.

Sometimes, short term only needs a start date. When you meet your goals, the intent is that you'll continue doing what you're doing from that point forward.

Here are some examples:

Short Term: *Starting tonight when the kids are in bed.*

Short Term: *By the end of the month.*

Short Term: *Within one week.*

Short-Term, Easy Goals

What does Easy Goals mean?

Easy Goals mean that your goals can be reached easily. In a sense, you're guaranteeing that you'll reach your goals.

Here are some examples:

Easy Goals: *Spend at least 10 minutes every day listening to my husband. No TV or other distractions.*

Easy Goals: *No more guessing. I'll ask more questions to sort out what he's saying.*

Easy Goals: *Spend time together on a new common interest we didn't know we had.*

Short-Term, Easy Goals

What does pay off mean?

Pay off means, when you reach each goal you've written there will be a benefit. The effort you put into even minor differences relating to your partner will have a positive pay off for you.

When you write a goal, ask yourself what achieving that goal will do for:

- Me_____

- My husband_____

- Our marriage_____

Back to an earlier example.

Short-Term, Easy Goal:
Spend at least 10 minutes every day listening to my wife. No TV or other distractions. Starting tonight when the kids are in bed.

What will be the Pay Off for me?
Learn more about her day and how she's doing and it will begin smoothing out how we interact.

What will be the Pay Off for my husband?
He'll know I care and it will make him feel more cared for.

What will be the Pay Off for our marriage?
Improve how we communicate and make us closer.

This book and the approach it presents, builds on good, and focuses on the action you will take, not what your husband will do.

When you do things differently to improve your marriage, your husband will react to those changes.

Creating 3 Short-Term, Easy Goals that Support My Priorities

1. Review your Action Plan and Priorities in Step One.

2. Develop 3 Short-Term, Easy Goals that relate to your top priorities.

3. Think what the pay offs will be and write them for each goal.

The example on the page at the right shows an Action Plan with Step Two completed.

Additional goals.
In time, your goals will become strengths and a natural part of you. When you meet one of your goals and it becomes "part of you," create new goals by checking the priority rankings from your Action Plan to help you select the next goal(s).

Keep just a few goals on your Action Plan at any one time. That keeps it manageable.

As you move forward and your marriage is strengthened, you may want to create goals that aren't part of your assessment from Step One, but evolve out of your day-to-day activities. That's good, do it!

Step Two – Action Plan - Example

Creating 3 Short-Term, Easy Goals That Support My Priorities

Priority: 1- Point of View (POV)
GOAL: Reduce our differences that cause arguments, by the 15th.

- ❏ Pay off for me: More interest in talking about the POV topics.

- ❏ Pay off for my husband: More confident in starting conversations.

- ❏ Pay off for our marriage: Easier to strive for common goals.

Priority: 2 - Interests
GOAL: Find something new we both want to do, in 2 weeks.

- ❏ Pay off for me: The fun of doing something new.

- ❏ Pay off for my husband: Excitement in doing something together.

- ❏ Pay off for our marriage: Activities that are fun to do and will bring us closer
  together.

Priority: 3 - Communication
GOAL: Make it through the day without tension, in one month.

- ❏ Pay off for me: Feel more like talking.

- ❏ Pay off for my husband: Peace of mind, less stress.

- ❏ Pay off for our marriage: Will open lines of communication.

Complete Step Two of Your Action Plan

1. Transfer your top 3 priorities to your Acton Plan.

2. Include the number and name of the priority.

3. Write 3 Short-Term, Easy Goals

4. Complete the pay offs section for each goal.

5. Double check what you've done to make sure it's what you want to say.

Step Two – Action Plan

Creating 3 Short-Term, Easy Goals That Support My Priorities

*Priority:*___ _____

*GOAL:*_____

- ❑ Pay off for me:_____
- ❑ Pay off for my husband:_____
- ❑ Pay off for our marriage:_____

*Priority:*___ _____

*GOAL:*_____

- ❑ Pay off for me:_____
- ❑ Pay off for my husband:_____
- ❑ Pay off for our marriage:_____

*Priority:*___ _____

*GOAL:*_____

- ❑ Pay off for me:_____
- ❑ Pay off for my husband:_____
- ❑ Pay off for our marriage:_____

Where Do We Go From Here?

Checking Your Progress

Great work! Another milestone. In Step One you determined your strengths, pinpointed areas for sharpening and set your priorities. Second, you set your direction by focusing on 3 Short-Term, Easy Goals and describing the pay offs.

It's important that you keep moving forward at this point. Don't lose momentum. Keep moving toward your future. You probably don't need to make earth-shattering changes. It's really a matter of taking small steps. The steps you take may be so small that you'll move forward almost without noticing. You might remember the story about the ant moving its hill, one grain of sand at a time. Improving your marriage is like moving one grain of sand at a time.

Selecting the Right Tools to Reach Your Goals

The tools you select in Step Three will help you move from where you are today toward your goals, so you can experience the pay offs. That's when you'll begin to realize that the picture of your future in your head is becoming a reality.

You already communicate or take actions in your marriage that would be considered "tools." Some tools you have are good and work well. Keep using them. Other tools are worn, chipped or rusty and don't work like they once did. Set them aside.

This book offers proven tools. Some are reminders and others are new ones that can be added to your good tools. And, as you might expect, there may be some empty spaces in your tool pouch that can be filled with specialized tools from other resources at a later date.

Step Three

Selecting the Right Tools to Reach Your Goals

Starting Point: Winning Action
Instructions

Absolutely Critical Tools
1. Action Now!
2. Three Must Do's
3. Tell Your Husband What's Important to You
4. Ask Your Husband What's Important to Him
5. Reframe

Face-to-Face
6. Emotional Continuum
7. Talking With Your Husband
8. Expand and Check
9. Balanced Feedback
10. Handle Differences
11. Common Sense Honesty
12. Red Flags

Lengthening a Short Fuse
13. Channeling Anger
14. Fighting Fair...?
15. Jettison Your Links to the Past

Staying on Track
16. Creating Success
17. Focus on Strengths
18. Work Around a Weakness

How's it Going?
19. Celebrate Any Improvements!
20. Thanks!

Completing Your Action Plan
- Selecting the Right Tools to Reach Your Goals

Where Do I Go From Here?
- Looking to the Future
- Commitment

Starting Point: Winning Action

Think of yourself as having a winning relationship. That means you're committed to strengthening your marriage in spite of the obstacles you may face. Once you commit, turn your back on the alternatives and distractions.

Your husband will respond to the positive action you take, maybe not overnight, but in time. When you have the determination to improve your marriage, you'll find time for productive action.

The most valuable asset you can ever own is an image of yourself as a woman who is a winner!

Therefore:
- Commit to winning action!
- Your future is in the best hands it could be: yours.

Selecting the Right Tools to Reach Your Goals

There are several sets of tools presented on the following pages that will help you meet your goals. Select only those tools, or parts of tools, you need to support your goals. Going forward, keep this book handy as a ready reference.

The tools in Step Three are numbered for easy reference, not by importance. They are put into a logical sequence and chunked into similar categories for ease of use and reference.

Tool format:

Left-hand page:
- Name of the tool
- Description
- Key Ideas

Right-hand page:
- Tips
- Recap

Estimated time to read the tools: 30 – 45 minutes.

1. Action Now!

Description
Action Now! reinforces the fact that timely action brings quick results.

Key Ideas

- Action Now! shows your husband that taking action, not just talking about it, is a top priority for you in improving your marriage.

- Lack of action translates into not caring.

- What if you decide to start next week? Or, in September once the kids are in school? Or, when you get that raise? Putting off action becomes a stall tactic.

- Positive actions straight away, not waiting until just the right time, show how serious you are about making things better.

- The action you take might be a very small step, but visible actions become the outward signs that give your husband confidence and trust in what you're doing, even if he doesn't say anything.

Absolutely Critical Tools

1. Action Now!

Tips

- Develop a sense of urgency for taking action to improve your marriage.

- The best time to start is now.

- Begin immediately, even if your first step is small.

Recap

Action Now! demonstrates in real ways, the love and commitment you have for your husband and your marriage.

2. Three Must Do's

Description

There are at least three basic ideas that are crucial to improving your marriage. Focus deliberately and consistently on these three must do's.

Key Ideas

- Give him caring treatment.

- Don't assume or guess.

- Don't play games.

2. Three Must Do's

Tips
Give him caring treatment.
- Be consistent in how you react to your husband.
- Be deliberate in showing that you care.
- Take time to do things right and completely.

Don't assume or guess.
- Ask questions to make sure you understand.
- Listen to what your husband is saying and not just what you want to hear.
- Get information out on the table so you're clear on what he's doing or thinking.

Don't play games.
- Games mean something else is going on deep inside one or both of you.
- Games get in the way of moving your marriage forward.
- Listening, taking time and steering clear of games, shows your husband that you value him. In turn, he will value you more.

Recap
No assumptions, no guessing, no games.

3. Tell Your Husband What's Important to You

Description
It's important that you tell your husband what's important to you and why. Give him clear and complete information to work with in understanding you.

Key Ideas
- Keep what's important to you limited to a critical few, such as 2 – 3 items so it doesn't seem like a mind dump.

- What's important can be centered on areas such as your marriage, the kids, work or the house, for example.

Be clear in your mind why "these certain things" are important to you. Be able to explain them to your husband.

3. Tell Your Husband What's Important to You

Tips

- Pick a good time and place to tell your husband what's important to you. It could be riding in the car, at the breakfast table Saturday morning before the kids get up or lying in bed in the dark. You'll know the best place.

- What you say might sound something like, "We were talking yesterday about the kids doing their homework late at night. What's important to me is that they do their homework before they get sleepy. What's important to you?"

- Formalize what's important to you. Write it down. Enter it into your computer or scratch it out on the back of an envelope, but make it permanent.

Recap

Tell your husband what's important to you.

4. Ask Your Husband What's Important to Him

Description

The simple question, "What's important to you?" sends a strong message to your husband. It says you care and are showing that you care by engaging in conversation to find out what matters.

Key Ideas

- Make sure you are totally clear on what's important to your husband.

- Make sure you understand why it's important to him without it becoming an interrogation.

4. Ask Your Husband What's Important to Him

Tips

There are two ways to ask your husband what's important to him:

1. General importance, with an open question, like: "We're going to the ball game with Bill and Jan; I'm looking forward to talking with Bill about the new players, what's important to you?"

2. Specific importance, like: "I know you like the new breakfast place on Elm Street, when we go there, what's important to you?"

Be ready to respond to what your husband says with statements like:

- "Tell me more."
- "Thanks for telling me, it helps me understand you better."
- "What else."

Recap

Ask your husband what's important to him.

5. Reframe

Description
Reframing is the ability to look at a situation differently.

Key Ideas

- We see what our mind tells us to see. In other words, we interpret actions, words and events through a series of filters that have been put in place over many years.

- A group of people seeing the same funny movie react differently. One person might chuckle, a few laugh, one person laughs hardest and another barely smiles. That's because the same information is evaluated differently by each person, based on the life experiences they hold. What we do without knowing it, is develop filters, barriers, a sense of right and wrong and a viewpoint about work, career, relationships, family, politics and men.

5. Reframe

Tips
Reframe the situation so you can find the good things.

Example
Situation: You've been ready for 15 minutes to meet your friends for dinner. Your husband still seems to be putzing around and that will make the two of you late for a nice evening out. He spent forever cleaning the garage, but now you'll be late. Isn't that just like him! The shower is going and the bathroom is steamed up and he hasn't even shaved yet! You're about to lose your cool.

Same situation reframed: He wants to look good for you.

Reframe it even more: Break the situation into parts:
- He's been busy all day and that's making him hustle now.
- He smells nice.
- He looks like he lost a bit of weight.
- He looks great in that new shirt.

Result: You meet your friends at 7:15 instead of 7:00, big deal.

Recap
Reframe what you're seeing and thinking into new positive views.

6. Emotional Continuum

Description

Almost on a daily basis at home, work or in a group, your emotions run up and down the emotional continuum. Even though you don't show it outwardly, there's always a reaction to what's happening to you. And, there's a reaction from your husband about how he's being treated by you.

+100

- **Spirit building**   You show energized support for your husband.
- **Connection**   You're in sync with your husband.
- **Validation**   You confirm that he has worth.
- **Acceptance**   You use positive words and body language.

Base Line

- **Indifference**   You show a clear lack of interest.
- **Rejection**   Your words and actions push your husband away.
- **Verbal shots**   Your words chip away at him.
- **Spirit killing**   Your words and action hammer your husband.

-100

Key Idea

- **Intent and Effect:** The intent of your words or actions may be positive in your mind, but the way it comes across to your husband, i.e., the effect, may be just the opposite.

- **Accumulated feelings:** The levels on the emotional continuum act like a cup that is filled and then spills over. A steady diet of indifference can add up to rejection. Or, a continued use of acceptance can become as positive as validation.

- **Stay above the base line:** Use communication and actions above the base line all the time.

6. Emotional Continuum

Tips

- Always stay above the base line in words and action in every single interaction with your husband.
  - ✓ Easy? No.
  - ✓ Necessary? Yes.

- Discipline yourself to stay above the base line.

- Be aware of your body language and tone of voice. You may be saying more than you think. For example, a look, shrugging your shoulders or speaking with a jagged edge to your voice can actually say more than your words.

- Your husband might speak and act below the base line. Separate issue. It's important that you work hard to stay above the line.

Recap
Stay above the base line.

7. Talking With Your Husband

Description

Clear balanced communication between you and your husband is an essential part of the strengthening process. It takes effort, concentration and persistence. The pay off is well worth the investment of your time.

Key Ideas

- Pay attention.

- When you're talking, be clear and make sense.

- Be aware of your body language, facial expressions and tone of voice.

7. Talking With Your Husband

Tips

- **Do:**
  - ✓ Listen totally and concentrate.
  - ✓ Listen to your husband's tone of voice.
  - ✓ Stay balanced and calm.
  - ✓ Use a warm tone of voice.
  - ✓ Be patient.
  - ✓ Let him know you're tuned in by your facial expression or subtle gestures or by saying things like, "mmm" or "uh-huh," or just nod.

- **Don't:**
  - ✓ Interrupt or rush the conversation.
  - ✓ Judge, get defensive or critical.
  - ✓ Ignore his feelings.
  - ✓ Withdraw and clam up.
  - ✓ Allow distractions like work or sports to run through your mind while listening to him.

Recap
Clear balanced communication is essential for growth.

8. Expand and Check

Description
Getting clear and complete information is important in communication. Meaningful thoughts and ideas can be reached by using expand and check.

Key Ideas
Expanding
Expanding on your husband's comments, opinions or suggestions is a way for you to get information. Sometimes the picture in his head is not being received in yours. You can expand on the "picture" he has by asking questions to obtain additional information.

Examples:
- "You think there's a problem with the car? Say more about that."

- "What do you mean?" (Be aware of your tone.)

- "I'm not sure I understand. Tell me more."

Checking
After listening to your husband, it's important to "check it out." That means tell husband what you heard. He'll let you know if it's correct. You don't have to agree with what he said; it just lets him know you understand.

Examples:
- "What you're saying is the new schedule we set up is actually taking longer unless one of us takes a shower before the kids take their bath. Is that right?"

- "You think the main benefit you see is saving time by using an on-line system."

8. Expand and Check

Tips
Sample conversation using expand and check.

Alex and Lisa have the monthly bills spread out on the table and Lisa is irritated.

Alex: "Come on Lisa, we don't need to go over these bills again, do we?

Lisa: "What do you mean?"

Alex: "We keep changing the priorities of what gets paid this week and I can't get a handle on how much money we'll have left over."

Lisa: "You're saying that continually going over the bills and changing priorities for what gets paid is driving you crazy?"

Alex: "Yes, that's it exactly."

Expanding and checking shows him that you have a clear picture of his view point, whether you agree or not. Using expand and check over time will establish a pattern that will encourage stronger discussions. Your husband will feel more valued when you listen and using expand and check also meets his need to connect.

Recap
First understand and then be understood.

9. Balanced Feedback

Description

To reach a positive result when you want something changed, let your husband know what you're thinking. Balanced feedback has proven to be one of the most effective ways to reach a positive outcome.

Your feedback must be relevant, appropriate and constructive. The purpose must be improvement, not blame. When delivered constructively, it won't be viewed as negative.

The determining factor in whether your wife is open to what you say or not, is how you present feedback.

Key Ideas

The feedback must be clear in two areas:
1. The positive "things" you want him to keep doing.
2. The difficulties and concerns to be improved.

This is the basis for the term balanced.

Example:

Lisa sees a long list of vacation activities on the table with big dollar signs floating in the air above them, and she knows they just don't have the money right now.

"Alex, you outlined our vacation down to the last detail; I like that (positive); but, I'm not sure we have the money for each activity (Lisa expresses her concern). How can we stay within budget and still do most of what you have on the vacation plan? Let's talk about some ideas to do that."

9. Balanced Feedback

Tips

Sample conversation using balanced feedback:

Lisa sees Alex getting frustrated with frequent changes to the kitchen remodeling plans.

Lisa: "Alex, I'd like to follow up on the plans for the kitchen. Your ideas are great. I'm concerned that you're getting frustrated with all the changes and not thinking your best"

Alex: "You're right Lisa; I am getting uptight and angry."

Lisa: "How can we get the good ideas out without all the frustration? How can I help?"

Alex: "I'd like to start from scratch?"

Lisa: "And?"

Alex: "Well, I have too many ideas. Maybe if I went back to square one, it would help. Just to clear my mind. Thanks for helping me sort it out."

Alex has calmed down and all Lisa did was use balanced feedback plus some expanding. The entire exchange took about 10 seconds, but the pay off will create many positives. It's a win-win approach.

Recap

Balanced feedback: keep the good, explain your concern and explore ideas for improvement.

10. Handle Differences

Description

As soon as you sense a difference between your views or thoughts and your husband's, it needs to be addressed. Don't wait. Early, small differences can mushroom and become complicated and out of control when not addressed soon enough. Too often, differences become the TNT in an argument and are blown completely out of proportion. That spells trouble.

Key Ideas

Handling a difference:

- Nip the difference while it's small!

- Tell your husband what's important to you and why you feel the way you do.

- Then, ask him what's important to him and why.

- Expand and check what he says to make sure you understand.

Once the difference is out and discussed, it may be enough. If there's still a difference, begin looking at options and new ideas. Use balanced feedback, along with expand and check as your tools to work through your differences.

Example:

Lisa: "What's important to me Alex is that I am able to go to our daughter's game. I want her to know that I support her activities because it means a lot to her. What's important to you?"

Alex: "I don't want to spend all day at the game."

Lisa: "Say more."

Alex: "We spend hours at the game, you talk with the other dads and in my mind I see all kinds of work at home not getting done."

Now Lisa knows the real issue and they can look for ways to address his need to be at the game as well as talk with other dads and Alex knows they'll explore ways to get the work done, also.

10. Handle Differences

Tips
Sample conversation using handling differences:

Lisa is sitting at the table Thursday after dinner and the weekend comes up in conversation.

Lisa: "Id like to go to your brother's this weekend Alex, but what's really important to me is that I have some time Saturday and Sunday to finish the projects I've started. What's important to you?"

Alex: "I still want to go to my brothers."

Lisa: "Say more." (Expanding because she still doesn't understand why.)

Alex: "My brother has redone the workshop. I'd like to see it."

Lisa: "Anything else?" (Expanding.)

Alex: "I like to see the kids playing with their cousins. They're becoming good ball players."

Lisa: "...and?" (More expanding.)

Alex: "I like to see you spending time with my sister-in-law. She likes you and it makes me feel good to see you two together."

Lisa: "I didn't think about it what way. What I can do is work on the major projects Saturday, go to your brother's with you and the kids on Sunday, and all of us can work on the remaining loose ends of the projects after work on Tuesday. How does that sound?"

Alex: "That'll work."

When you have the right information and take time to get at the core of the issue, a difference can be handled in a productive manner.

Recap
Handle differences while they're small.

11. Common Sense Honesty

Description

Being honest is telling the truth and not withholding information. But, it must be done with common sense and sensitivity, and it must be guided by your desire to strengthen your marriage.

Key Ideas

- Honesty can only take place when there is trust in your relationship.

- Being honest allows your husband to express his opinion without fear of criticism from you.

- Being honest allows you to express your opinion without criticism from him.

- Being honest erases any doubts your husband has about what you're communicating.

- Being honest doesn't mean being cruel or hurtful.

11. Common Sense Honesty

Tips

Practice being honest with easier, more straightforward areas first.

Example: Your husband says, "Would you go out to the hardware and pick up some nails for me?"

- Old way: "No, I'm too busy."

- Message to him: That he isn't important, i.e., below the base line.

- New way, being honest: "I'm right in the middle of this project and it's important to me that I finish it tonight."

- Message to him: You're trying to complete a project. Now he has a better picture in his mind and won't take it so negatively.

Choose your words carefully when talking with him, but be honest.

Example: He asks if you want to go to his brother's with him.

- Old way: "No."

- Message to her: That he isn't important, and you may not like her brother or he makes up reasons in his head.

- New way, being honest: "I always feel like I'm on the fringe when the two of you talk about sports and cars all the time. I'd rather just stay here and get caught up on the yard work."

- Message to him: He still knows you don't want to go, but now he also knows why, because you're being honest and not withholding information.

Recap

Be honest with common sense.

12. Red Flags

Description

Red flags are those high-risk situations that develop over time between you and your husband. They just do. It happens to almost everyone. To strengthen your marriage, it's important to react differently to those old situations that had, and continue to have, negative outcomes. How? By using a new reaction you've prepared in advance.

Key Ideas

- Red flags have a history.

- They trigger a reaction.

- They can escalate from 0 – 60 in a nanosecond.

- Solution: have a positive pre-planned reaction, set to go.

12. Red Flags

Tips

Don't give in to the short term pay off by going back to your old ways that sometimes makes you temporarily feel good.

You already know what will happen when you act in the old ways: throwing gasoline on the fire. Have a pre-planned solution ready.

Here's the plan:
- Old way: Trigger-------------------------------------Old reaction.
- New way: Same trigger---------pre-set plan----------New reaction

Example 1, Old way:
- Situation: Clothing.

- Trigger: He says, "You're not going to wear that sweater, are you?"

- Old reaction, using sarcasm: "No, just wanted to see if it still fits."

- Old reaction, just going along: You mumble comments under your breath just loud enough for him to hear, as you walk toward the closet. You already know from plenty of past experience that your mumbled comments will escalate into the next level of intensity.

Example 2. New way:
- New reaction, (being aware of your tone and body language) using the pre-set plan of expanding: "Say more."

- Pre-set plan: Use expand.

- He says, "That sweater doesn't go well with those slacks and it makes you look older."

- You, "I didn't think about that." And you rummage about in the closet looking for another shirt-slack combination.

- Or, you could say, "Thanks for telling me. I'll change the sweater."

Recap
Pre-set plan = new reaction.

13. Channeling Anger

Description

Anger is a feeling that builds up in side you and creates a sense of pressure to do something, to take action, and as a result, you snap! It may be verbal or physical aggression. As your anger continues to build, your husband may seem like an opponent. You might treat him in ways you'll regret later. For both of you, the negative thoughts that develop can act like filters, keeping out any positive attempts to "smooth things over."

Anger can become serious and damaging with little hope of regaining what was lost.

Key Ideas

- Anger can be shown in two basic ways:
    - ✓ **Constructive:** dealing with the triggers of your anger in the right way.
    - ✓ **Destructive:** your anger turns into an attack on your husband.

- When one spouse is controlled by the other's anger, they'll usually get their power back in some way.

- To some extent, anger and/or conflict exist in most marriages. How those feelings are dealt with determines much of the success or failure of a marriage.

13. Channeling Anger

Tips

- If your anger is causing problems in your marriage, make a commitment to yourself that you'll handle your anger differently.

- Have a pre-set plan in mind to deal with your anger in constructive ways.

- Set limits of what you won't accept from your husband, when dealing with anger and talk with him about it.

- Avoid escalating your anger and argument just to win!

- Stay in the present, not the past or future.

- Call "Time Out" just like in a hectic basketball game. It's to get some space.

- You could say, "I'm going outside for 10 minutes." Saying that sends a strong message to him that you really do care and are willing to do something differently.

- You might simply agree on a time to continue talking.

- "Let's take a break before things get out of hand. How about getting back together tonight so we can discuss this constructively."

Recap
Channel anger constructively.

14. Fighting Fair...?

Description

Fighting is when you cross the line from the issue and go after your husband with words or actions directed at him personally.

Key Ideas

- **DON'T FIGHT**

- No one wins in a fight. The issue becomes worse and you often end up further apart.

- Disagreeing, having passion or conflict isn't fighting.

- Your disagreement becomes a fight when you get off the issue you're talking about and attack your husband.

- Deal with the issue. Don't dredge up hurtful names or make derogatory comments.

14. Fighting Fair...?

Tips

- Open the door for a different approach by saying something like, "I want to resolve the issue, not fight."

- Don't fight in front of the kids, family, relatives or in public.

- Stick to the issue!

- If one of you begins to attack personally, get a grip and bring the discussion back to the issue.

- Get to the point, but use common sense and tact.

- Look for solutions.

- Be patient.

- Listen.

- Expand and check. It's hard to expand and check when you're heated, but do it anyway.

- Use balanced feedback, also.

- Use handle differences.

- End with something positive.

Recap

No one wins in a fight.

15. Jettison Your Links to The Past

Description
Links to the past are situations that have caused problems between you and him before they resurface when you become angry. Links to the past can be pulled up and deliberately used to hurt.

Key Ideas
- Old links come from a totally different script out of the past.

- Get rid of old thoughts.

- The past is past. You can't change what happened but you can change how you react to what happened.

- Don't keep packing old baggage. Let it go.

- If you don't make some effort toward dumping the old links, you'll revisit them over and over again in your future.

15. Jettison Your Links to The Past

Tips

Stop bringing up old links like:

- "What about the name you called me?" (10 years ago.)

- "You always embarrass me in front of my friends." (New Years Eve, 2002)

- "You don't even care how well I do any repairs around the house." (A project last summer.)

To you, old comments can seem like moments ago, but it's counter-productive to pull them up when you're strengthening your marriage.

Replace your old scripts with new statements. Keep new thoughts in your head like:

- "I want to improve our marriage."

- "Sure, there will be bumps along the road, but we're going forward."

- "We've had issues, but we have to look to the future."

- To yourself: "Don't forget my Short-Term, Easy Goals and the Pay Off we'll get."

Recap

Dump the baggage you've been slogging around.

16. Creating Success

Description

You've heard, "Nothing succeeds like success." You could easily make a list of the times at work, activities or with friends when you've experienced successes that laid the foundation for more successes. It's important that, in your marriage, you create some measure of success, however small, as often as you can.

Key Ideas

- Small positive efforts bring big results.

- Start with something you know will work. It serves as an anchor and kick starts the momentum you're trying to gain.

- Keep searching for more ways and ideas to create success.

16. Creating Success

Tips

- Look for the positives in something your husband does, every day. Athletic coaches do it with players. Acknowledge what's he'd doing well, "That new seasoning on the meat is great!" Just that simple.

- Your husband can never hear enough of what he's doing right. Keep telling him even if it seems silly.

- Spend time every day focusing on your husband. Show affection through words and action.

- Do the research and develop a more complete, caring and sensitive lovemaking style.

- Support each other's interests by listening closely, with undivided attention if only for 5 minutes!

- Take time to listen to his problems without trying to solve them. He may need to talk about it. This easy, no cost action is one approach for deepening his feelings of trust and safety in you.

- Let him know you appreciate his efforts. That'll work wonders.

- Do more little things for him rather than only a big event once in a while.

- Work for results, not praise. Praise will follow on its own.

- Put your antennae up. Anticipate what he needs.

- If you pursue your interests, make sure you also take time for him. In a word: balance!

Recap

Success creates more success.

17. Focus on Strengths

Description

Your personal strengths and the strengths currently in your marriage are the cornerstones of your future. It's important to be clear about your strengths and use them to put together a chain of positives.

Key Ideas

- Strengths provide a solid foundation upon which you can continue to build upon.

- Several strengths together give a total that's more than any of the strengths by themselves. The formula: $2 + 2 = 5$.

- You will be faced with challenges as you move forward. Solid, reliable strengths provide a strong footing.

17. Focus on Strengths

Tips

- Be consistent and deliberate in your ability to identify strengths.

- Build on any strengths you can.

- Keep your strengths right up front!

- Keep noting strengths already present in your marriage, no matter how small they may seem.

- Write down your strengths from Step One in this book, as well as anything else you can think of that's positive about your marriage.

Recap
Focus on the strengths in your marriage.

18. Work around a Weakness

Description

Even the best plan for entertaining on the weekend, has weaknesses. The perfect marriage has weaknesses. And, just like when you entertain, you or your marriage may have areas that cause concerns and they just won't go away.

Key Ideas

- There are some weaknesses you can't do anything about.

- If you keep trying to change a weakness, the effort may become counterproductive.

- Acknowledge the fact that either you or your marriage may have a weakness.

- Sometimes you'll have to find a way to work around a weakness.

18. Work around a Weakness

Tips
Example 1
You can't leave work until 5 p.m. Your commute home is an hour. You and your spouse would like to eat as a family at 5:30 p.m., so your 1st and 2nd grade kids can do homework and be in bed by 8 p.m. You simply can't meet that schedule.

Work around it by exploring alternatives, such as:
- Suggest that the kids have an after-school snack to hold them until 6 p.m.

- Work on homework with them when you get home and eat dinner with your partner later.

- The kids eat while you're commuting. You help them with their homework and get them ready for bed while your spouse fixes a special dinner for the two of you.

Example 2
Your husband is just not organized. Never was, and it seems like he will never be organized. You see it as a weakness.

Work around it by:
- Reframing the situation and focusing on the strengths your husband has.

- Acknowledging that it may just be a "style" he carries.

- Some men take on too much and get overwhelmed. Offer to help with a few things to reduce the feeling of being overwhelmed.

- Help create structure around key activities to help him be more organized.

- Keep it in perspective. With all that is going on in the world, how important are her organizational skills? If important, then you have to work around the weakness by being part of the solution and use the tools provided in this book.

Recap
Work around a weakness.

19. Celebrate Any Improvement!

Description

We celebrate our kid's achievements. We celebrate when we get a raise at work. We celebrate our favorite sports teams. Why not celebrate any forward progress with your marriage? That means any improvement that you've noticed: small, medium or large.

Celebration is rewarding yourself for the good feelings that have surfaced because of your efforts at strengthening your marriage. Something is different now in your marriage and celebrating is a way of locking it in.

Key Ideas

- Celebration is a symbol of achievement.

- Any positives count!

- What have you noticed in your marriage that's going better now?

- Write down what the improvements have done for your marriage.

- Don't keep a running total, just note it.

- Have others noticed differences and commented to you?

- Have the kids said anything about how you guys are acting differently?

19. Celebrate Any Improvement!

Tips

- Think of doing something special: dinner, movie, etc.

- Here's what celebration comes down to: Action Now!

- You don't have to announce what you're doing as celebration. Just do it.

- You might celebrate by simply giving each other back rubs.

- For many people, it's the smaller day-to-day gestures that go the furthest.

Recap
Celebrate!

20. Thanks!

Description

This may be a blinding glimpse of the obvious; saying, "Thanks" is not only polite, but it is a way of letting your husband know you think he is important, and what he does is important.

You may think "Thank you.", but he needs to hear you say it.

Key Ideas

- Look your wife in the eyes.

- Be sincere.

- Smile.

20. Thanks!

Tips

Saying "Thanks" can be done is several ways, and may sound something like:

- "Thanks for taking care of the lawn, it really looks good."

- "I know you're pulled in many directions, but the kids and I appreciate how you work hard for us."

- "I don't say this often enough, but it's on my mind a lot. You're important to me and I just wanted to say how much I love you and appreciate how you take care of things around the house. Thank you."

Recap

Say "Thanks!"

Completing Your Action Plan

Selecting the Right Tools to Reach My Goals

You've done a lot to get to this point. You've identified the strengths already present in your marriage and you've set priorities for the areas you want to strengthen. That's great!

You wrote the pay offs that you'll experience when your goals are met. That step actually "painted the picture" of how you'd like your marriage to be in the future for those targeted areas. Not many couples do that. You'll discover a big pay off for that alone.

Well done!

You've either read thoroughly or at least leafed through the tools. For some goals you may select several tools, for other goals you may select a single tool or even parts of a tool.

You can always add more tools from other sources. Clip, staple, tape or type and place them in with your other tools. At times, you might select a tool, but in reality not use it. That happens. Find what works for you.

The example at the right shows an Action Plan with Step Three completed.

Estimated time to complete Step Three on your Action Plan: 15 – 45 minutes.

Step Three - Action Plan - Example

Selecting the Right Tools to Reach My Goals

Goal: Reduce our differences that cause arguments, by the 15th.
Tools I'll use and action I'll take to meet my goals.

- ❏ What's Important — Tell him what's important to me about my POV

- ❏ Expand/Check — Make sure I'm clear about what's important to him

- ❏ Common Sense Honesty — Be honest about my views, but tactful

Goal: Find something new we both want to do, in 2 weeks.
Tools I'll use and action I'll take to meet my goals.

- ❏ Action Now! — Take the initiative, don't wait

- ❏ Focus on Strengths — Build on our interest in nature

- ❏ Creating Success — Plan a day trip to the lake, just for us

Goal: Make it through the day without tension, in one month.
Tools I'll use and action I'll take to meet my goals.

- ❏ Channel Anger — #6, call time out - but do it right!

- ❏ Expand and Check — Say things like. "Tell me more."

- ❏ Emotional Continuum — Stay above the baseline

- ❏ Jettison Past Links — Focus on the future – erase the old tapes

Note:
- ❏ The last goal above has four tools. Any goal can have as many tools as it needs, from one to several!
- ❏ Or, as in channel anger, #6 from Tips was selected, not the entire tool.
- ❏ Here's the key: do what works, it can be changed; make adjustments wherever you need to make them. Just like other normal activities.

Complete Step Three of Your Action Plan

- Review your goals.

- Select tools or parts of tools you want to use to help you reach your goals.

- Add as many tools as you need. Just keep it manageable.

- Double check the tools you've selected; are they the ones that will work best for you?

Step Three – Action Plan

Selecting the Right Tools to Reach My Goals

*Goal:*_____

Tools I'll use and action I'll take to meet my goals.

     ❏ _____

     ❏ _____

     ❏ _____

     ❏ _____

*Goal:*_____

Tools I'll use and action I'll take to meet my goals.

     ❏ _____

     ❏ _____

     ❏ _____

     ❏ _____

*Goal:*_____

Tools I'll use and action I'll take to meet my goals.

     ❏ _____

     ❏ _____

     ❏ _____

     ❏ _____

Completed Action Plan - Example

The page at the right shows a completed one-page Action Plan.
The benefit of one page is that you can see everything at once.

Step One: Identifying My Strengths, Areas to Sharpen and Setting Priorities

	Strengths	Areas To Sharpen		Priorities
		Working on this will be: **EASY/Difficult**	The pay off will be: **BIG/Small**	
1. Chemistry	(S)	__/__	__/__	___
2. Interests	S	X/__	__/X	2
3. Communication	S	__/X	X/__	3
4. Social Compatibility	S	__/X	__/X	4
5. Intimacy	(S)	__/__	__/__	___
6. Point of View	S	X/__	X/__	1
7. Money	(S)	__/__	__/__	___
8. Self-Care	S	__/X	__/X	4
9. Meeting Needs	S	__/X	X/__	3
10. Underlying Currents	S	__/X	X/__	3
11. Quiet Moments	S	X/__	__/X	2
12. Your History Together	(S)	__/__	__/__	___

Step Two: Creating 3 Short-Term, Easy Goals That Support My Priorities, and Step Three: Selecting The Right Tools To Reach My Goals

Priority: 1- Point of View (POV)
GOAL: Reduce our differences that lead to tension, by the 15th.
- ❑ Pay off for me: More interest in talking about the POV topics.
- ❑ Pay off for my husband: More confident in making decisions.
- ❑ Pay off for our marriage: Easier to strive for common goals.

Tools I'll use and action I'll take to meet my goal.
- ❑ What's Important   Tell him what's important to me about POV
- ❑ Expand/Check   Make sure I'm clear on what's important to him
- ❑ Common Sense Honesty   Be honest about my views, but tactful

Priority: 2 - Interests
GOAL: Find something new we both want to do, in 2 weeks.
- ❑ Pay off for me: The fun of doing something new.
- ❑ Pay off for my husband: Excitement in doing something together.
- ❑ Pay off for our marriage: Activities to look forward to.

Tools I'll use and action I'll take to meet my goal.
- ❑ Action Now!   Take the initiative, don't wait
- ❑ Focus on Strength   Build on our interest in nature
- ❑ Creating Success   Plan a day trip to the lake, just for us

Priority: 3 - Communication
GOAL: Make it through the day without a fight, in one month.
- ❑ Pay off for me: Feel more like talking.
- ❑ Pay off for my husband: Peace of mind, less stress.
- ❑ Pay off for our marriage: Opens lines of communication.

Tools I'll use and action I'll take to meet my goal.
- ❑ Channel Anger   #6, call time out, but do it right
- ❑ Expand and Check   Make and keep a cheat sheet in my purse
- ❑ Emotional Continuum   Stay above the baseline
- ❑ Jettison Past Links   Focus on the future – erase the old tapes

Where Do I Go From Here?

Look to The Future

Every once in a while---weekly, every 2 weeks, but not longer---take a moment to check how you're doing. Formally, if you want, or thinking over a cup of coffee at the local café, but take a look at your Action Plan and note your progress.

If a goal is already met, create a new one so you always have three at any one time.

There are several blank Action Plans included in this book. Use them. You have permission to copy as many as you need.

Keep your old Action Plans so you can look back and see where you've been and prove to yourself that you're gaining ground on how you want your marriage to be.

You've accomplished a lot. Keep at it.

Commitment

Commit to your husband every day by giving him:
- Focused attention.
- Acceptance.
- Affection.

What Other's Have Said

"For the first time in a long time, I have hope that our marriage will work out."
Jan, Chicago, IL

"This is a familiar process; we use something like this at work."
Ted, St. Charles, IL

"This is good, quick hits."
Tom, Portland, OR

"I don't know what you guys did in the workshop last night, but my husband was nice twice this morning."
Nancy, Galesburg, IL

"I talked with my son for the first time in months."
Charlie, Houston, TX

"These ideas have helped my marriage and I use the tools with my kids and a couple of the tools at work."
Barb, Chelmsford, MA

"The tools are practical and straight forward."
Denny, USMC
Danville, IL

"Lock and load. I'm ready."
Kirk, Ph.D. and former combat Marine.
Chicago, IL

"I never had the chance to learn this kind of information before, it's really good!"
Pam, Champaign, IL

25 Insights

1. Build on good.
2. You're 50% in charge of the relationship.
3. You're 100% in charge of what you do.
4. Commit to winning action.
5. Action Now!
6. No assumptions, no guessing, no games, just caring.
7. Tell your husband what's important to you.
8. Ask your husband what's important to him.
9. Reframe.
10. Stay above the baseline.
11. Clear and balanced communication.
12. First understand and then be understood.
13. Keep the good things and explore ideas to improve.
14. Handle differences while they're small.
15. Be honest, with common sense.
16. Pre-set plan = new reaction.
17. Channel anger constructively.
18. No one wins in a fight.
19. Dump the baggage.
20. Success creates more success.
21. Focus on strengths.
22. Work around a weakness.
23. Celebrate.
24. Saying thanks.
25. Commitment.

3 Quick and Easy Steps Tool Grid

Action Now!	Three Must Do's	Tell What's Important	Ask What's Important
Reframe	Emotional Continuum	Talking With Your Partner	Expand and Check
Balanced Feedback	Handle Differences	Common Sense Honesty	Red Flags
Channeling Anger	Fighting Fair…?	Jettison Your Links to the Past	Creating Success
Focus on Strengths	Work Around a Weakness	Celebrate Any Improvements!	Thanks!

About The Author

Randall Krug is a parent, writer, seminar leader and coach. For over 20 years he has conducted hundreds of communication and leadership seminars in the business world, nationally and internationally. He served four years in the United States Navy and earned both a B.A and M.A. from Michigan State University. He coached rugby at both the Super League and All-America levels.

The frankness and practicality of Randall's background comes through in his writing and seminars. As many participants have said, "It's refreshing to get to the core ideas that make sense, and walk away with something I can use, now!"

He is an entertaining, challenging and inspiring writer and seminar leader.

Randall is founder and president of Personal Insights.

Personal Insights is a company that provides high-quality learning resources to help individuals improve their lives and thereby, the lives of others.

Personal Insights offers clearly written books, self-discovery tools that are backed by 30 years of proven reliability with over 40 million users and a range of practical seminars that strengthen interpersonal relationships.

3 Blank Action Plans

You may copy as many of these as you need.

Refer to **http://www.lulu.com/spotlight/krughauspublishing** if you'd like additional copies of this book or other resources.

ACTION PLAN

Step One: Identifying My Strengths, Areas to Sharpen and Setting Priorities

	Strengths	Areas To Sharpen		Priorities
		Working on this will be: **EASY/Difficult**	The pay off will be: **BIG/Small**	
		__/__	__/__	
1. Chemistry	S	__/__	__/__	__
2. Interests	S	__/__	__/__	__
3. Communication	S	__/__	__/__	__
4. Social Compatibility	S	__/__	__/__	__
5. Intimacy	S	__/__	__/__	__
6. Point of View	S	__/__	__/__	__
7. Money	S	__/__	__/__	__
8. Self-Care	S	__/__	__/__	__
9. Meeting Needs	S	__/__	__/__	__
10. Underlying Currents	S	__/__	__/__	__
11. Quiet Moments	S	__/__	__/__	__
12. Our History Together	S	__/__	__/__	__

Step Two: Creating 3 Short-Term, Easy Goals That Support My Priorities, and Step Three: Selecting The Right Tools To Reach My Goals

*Priority:*_____

GOAL: _____

    ❑ Pay off for me: _____

    ❑ Pay off for my husband: _____

    ❑ Pay off for our marriage: _____

Tools I'll use and action I'll take to meet my goals.

    ❑ _____ _____

    ❑ _____ _____

    ❑ _____ _____

*Priority:*_____

GOAL: _____

    ❑ Pay off for me: _____

    ❑ Pay off for my husband: _____

    ❑ Pay off for our marriage: _____

Tools I'll use and action I'll take to meet my goals.

    ❑ _____ _____

    ❑ _____ _____

    ❑ _____ _____

*Priority:*_____

GOAL: _____

    ❑ Pay off for me: _____

    ❑ Pay off for my husband: _____

    ❑ Pay off for our marriage: _____

Tools I'll use and action I'll take to meet my goals.

    ❑ _____ _____

    ❑ _____ _____

    ❑ _____ _____

ACTION PLAN

Step One: Identifying My Strengths, Areas to Sharpen and Setting Priorities

	Strengths	Areas To Sharpen		Priorities
		Working on this will be: **EASY/Difficult**	The pay off will be: **BIG/Small**	
		__/__	__/__	__
1. Chemistry	S	__/__	__/__	__
2. Interests	S	__/__	__/__	__
3. Communication	S	__/__	__/__	__
4. Social Compatibility	S	__/__	__/__	__
5. Intimacy	S	__/__	__/__	__
6. Point of View	S	__/__	__/__	__
7. Money	S	__/__	__/__	__
8. Self-Care	S	__/__	__/__	__
9. Meeting Needs	S	__/__	__/__	__
10. Underlying Currents	S	__/__	__/__	__
11. Quiet Moments	S	__/__	__/__	__
12. Our History Together	S	__/__	__/__	__

Step Two: Creating 3 Short-Term, Easy Goals That Support My Priorities, and Step Three: Selecting The Right Tools To Reach My Goals

*Priority:*_____

GOAL: _____

    ❑ Pay off for me: _____

    ❑ Pay off for my husband: _____

    ❑ Pay off for our marriage: _____

Tools I'll use and action I'll take to meet my goals.

    ❑ _____   _____

    ❑ _____   _____

    ❑ _____   _____

*Priority:*_____

GOAL: _____

    ❑ Pay off for me: _____

    ❑ Pay off for my husband: _____

    ❑ Pay off for our marriage: _____

Tools I'll use and action I'll take to meet my goals.

    ❑ _____   _____

    ❑ _____   _____

    ❑ _____   _____

*Priority:*_____

GOAL: _____

    ❑ Pay off for me: _____

    ❑ Pay off for my husband: _____

    ❑ Pay off for our marriage: _____

Tools I'll use and action I'll take to meet my goals.

    ❑ _____   _____

    ❑ _____   _____

    ❑ _____   _____

    ❑

Step One: Identifying My Strengths, Areas to Sharpen and Setting Priorities

	Strengths	Areas To Sharpen		Priorities
		Working on this will be:	The pay off will be:	
		EASY/Difficult	**BIG/Small**	
		__/__	__/__	
1. Chemistry	S	__/__	__/__	___
2. Interests	S	__/__	__/__	___
3. Communication	S	__/__	__/__	___
4. Social Compatibility	S	__/__	__/__	___
5. Intimacy	S	__/__	__/__	___
6. Point of View	S	__/__	__/__	___
7. Money	S	__/__	__/__	___
8. Self-Care	S	__/__	__/__	___
9. Meeting Needs	S	__/__	__/__	___
10. Underlying Currents	S	__/__	__/__	___
11. Quiet Moments	S	__/__	__/__	___
12. Our History Together	S	__/__	__/__	___

Step Two: Creating 3 Short-Term, Easy Goals That Support My Priorities, and Step Three: Selecting The Right Tools To Reach My Goals

*Priority:*_____

GOAL: _____

- ❏ Pay off for me: _____
- ❏ Pay off for my husband: _____
- ❏ Pay off for our marriage: _____

Tools I'll use and action I'll take to meet my goals.

- ❏ _____ _____
- ❏ _____ _____
- ❏ _____ _____

*Priority:*_____

GOAL: _____

- ❏ Pay off for me: _____
- ❏ Pay off for my husband: _____
- ❏ Pay off for our marriage: _____

Tools I'll use and action I'll take to meet my goals.

- ❏ _____ _____
- ❏ _____ _____
- ❏ _____ _____

*Priority:*_____

GOAL: _____

- ❏ Pay off for me: _____
- ❏ Pay off for my husband: _____
- ❏ Pay off for our marriage: _____

Tools I'll use and action I'll take to meet my goals.

- ❏ _____ _____
- ❏ _____ _____
- ❏ _____ _____

Made in the USA
Monee, IL
23 January 2022

89669464R00057